The Respiratory System

Justin Lee

the rosen publishing group's
rosen
central

To Courtney, for saving my life and being my friend.

Published in 2001 by The Rosen Publishing Group, Inc.
29 East 21st Street, New York, NY 10010

First Edition

Library of Congress Cataloging-in-Publication Data

Lee, Justin.
The respiratory system / Justin Lee. — 1st ed.
    p. cm. — (The insider's guide to the body)
  Includes bibliographical references and index.
  Summary: Discusses what the respiratory system is, how it works, and how it may be affected by various diseases.
  ISBN 0-8239-3335-0 (library binding)
   1. Respiratory organs—Juvenile literature. 2. Respiration—Juvenile literature. [1. Respiratory system. 2. Respiration.] I. Title. II. Series.
QP121. .L335 2000
612.2—dc21

                                00-009101

Manufactured in the United States of America

Contents

1
What Is the Respiratory System?

Ariana jogged down the soccer field, her white shorts and Blue Devils jersey heavy with sweat. Coach MacAffee called her to the sidelines, and she was happy to go. She had been playing right forward for the first three-quarters of the game. She had one goal and two assists. Her team was up four to three, and she was tired.

As she got to the sideline, the coach patted her back. "Good job, Ariana, way to play. Take a breather." Ariana started walking and then doubled over, resting her elbows on her knees. She was breathing hard. She straightened out her body and felt her lungs fill with air. The air rushed out again rapidly. She was breathing through her mouth and her nose, trying to get air. The coach held out Ariana's inhaler. Ariana put it to her mouth and breathed in the mist. Slowly she felt the air coming into her lungs more easily. She started breathing only through her nose. The cold November air hurt her lungs when she breathed through her mouth.

Dennis, Ariana's dad, sat on the bleachers cheering on his daughter. He knew that she would be out for only a minute. As

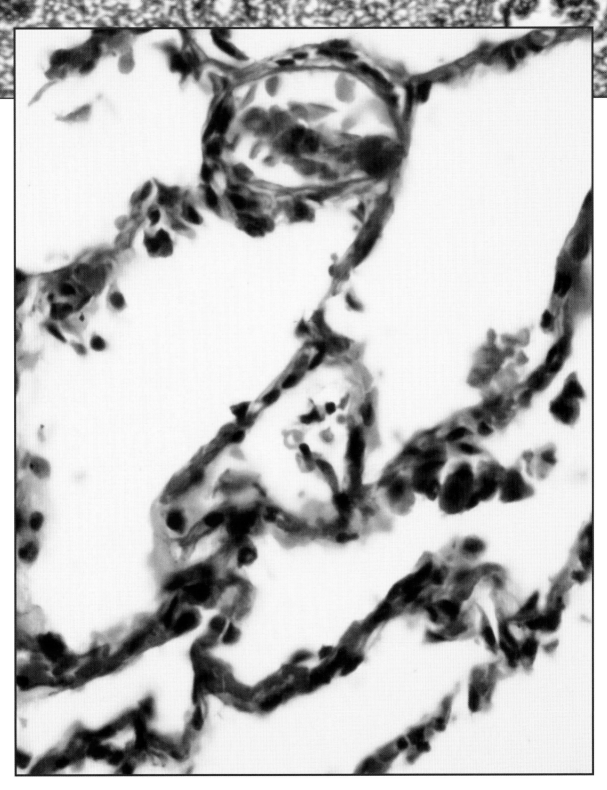

This is a close-up view of the air sacs and capillaries of the lung tissue.

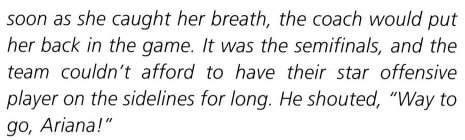

soon as she caught her breath, the coach would put her back in the game. It was the semifinals, and the team couldn't afford to have their star offensive player on the sidelines for long. He shouted, "Way to go, Ariana!"

Suddenly the other team drove down the field. The girl out in front seemed to dodge every defender that tried to take the ball from her. She kept the ball tightly inside her step and took it all the way down. Ariana saw the goalie, Karen, try to position herself to block the shot. It was no good, the opponent was too fast—she kicked a perfect ball into the high right side of the net. Karen jumped, but it was too late. The game was now tied four to four. Coach MacAffee looked at Ariana. "Are you ready? Can you go back in?" he asked. "I know you haven't had enough rest, but the team needs you." Ariana smiled and took a slow deep breath. She said she was ready, and the coach signaled Liz to come out. Ariana ran back on the field.

A lot of people like to play some kind of sport. Even those who don't play sports like to talk, or yell, or move their bodies. Every time we breath, cough, sneeze, laugh, speak, move, cry, or sing, we use our respiratory system. We wouldn't be able to live more than a few minutes without it. It works all night while we sleep. It starts functioning when we are born and keeps working until we die, never taking a break.

The respiratory system is made up of your lungs, the tubes that connect your lungs to the outside air, and the part of your circulatory system that allows your blood to absorb, or pick up, the oxygen from your lungs. However, there is a lot more to your respiratory system than just your lungs and some tubes. It is an amazingly complex system. It is linked to your brain, your heart, even to your bones and muscles. It relies on special muscles that allow your lungs to expand and contract. Simply put, your respiratory system allows you to breathe, and breathing allows you to speak, move, and live.

Inhalation and Exhalation

When you inhale, you breathe in, and when you exhale you breathe out. The air we breathe in contains a lot of oxygen, which our bodies need to survive. In fact, all animals need oxygen in order to live. The air we breathe out contains less oxygen and more carbon dioxide, which is a gas our bodies produce as a waste product. Since the carbon dioxide is poisonous, we need to get it out of our bodies. Our respiratory system does this during exhalation. The process of inhalation and exhalation—when oxygen is absorbed and carbon dioxide is expelled— is called respiration.

Inhalation allows for the absorption of oxygen into the body, while exhalation forces carbon dioxide out.

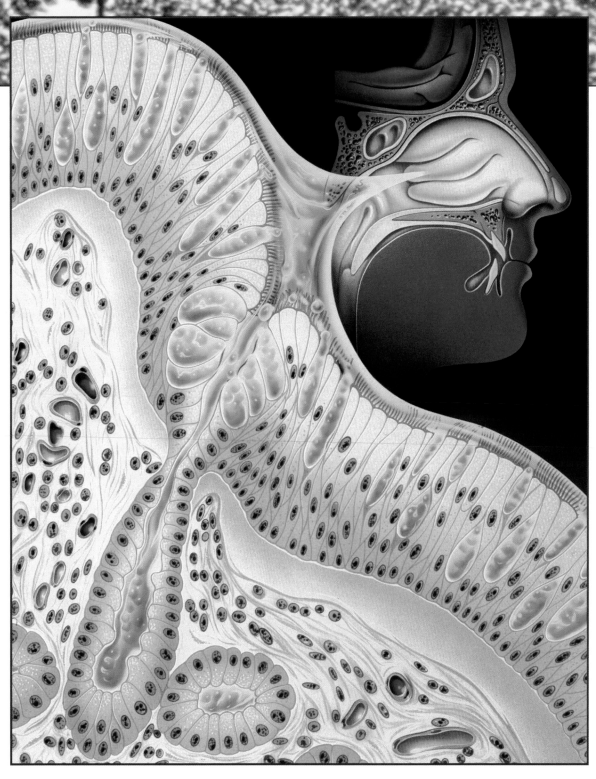

The nasal cavity is a system of airways that allows air to travel
to and from the lungs.

Lungs and Your Brain, Heart, and Muscles

An average adult can take more than eighty breaths per minute when he or she is exercising. However, the same adult takes only between twelve and twenty breaths per minute when he or she is resting.

Our lungs don't work all by themselves. In fact, they are completely helpless on their own. The lungs are very complex organs. They are two spongy, saclike organs inside the chest that hold air. They can't expand or contract by themselves; they can't even decide when the body needs more or less air. The lungs hold the air while oxygen and carbon dioxide are exchanged, but other parts of the body control how much air is taken in, how much carbon dioxide is expelled, and how the oxygen gets from the lungs to the rest of the body. To breathe, the systems of the body must work together.

The lungs inflate like balloons so that air can rush into them, and they deflate to push the air out. But the lungs don't have any muscles of their own. Because of this, other muscles do the work for them—the diaphragm and ribs work together to inflate and deflate the lungs. When your body needs more air, the ribs move outward, widening the space inside your chest, which is called the chest cavity. At the same time, the diaphragm, which is a dome-shaped muscle that divides the chest cavity from the abdominal cavity (the space inside your belly), moves down and increases the depth of the chest cavity. As the space inside the chest increases, air swells the lungs and we inhale. When we need to exhale, the diaphragm moves up and the ribs move in, squeezing air out of the lungs.

Another thing your lungs need help with is knowing how often to inflate and deflate. Sometimes—for example, when you are running—your lungs have to work quickly. At other times— like when you are sleeping—they need to work more slowly. But lungs have no way of knowing how much oxygen is being used or how hard you are working. Your lungs depend on the brain to know when to get more air and when to slow down. Your lungs and the muscles of your diaphragm are linked to the part of your nervous system that figures out how much oxygen you need to take in and how much carbon dioxide you need to get rid of. The nervous system tells the respiratory system to either speed up or slow down, making sure the body takes in the right amount of oxygen.

Your lungs are also very closely linked to your heart—so closely linked that the heart and lungs are often referred to as one system. Your lungs take the oxygen out of the air you breathe in. The lungs also push poisonous carbon dioxide out of the body when you breathe out. But how does the carbon dioxide get to your lungs in the first place, and where does the oxygen go once the lungs have absorbed it from the air? The answer to both of these questions is the heart. We will learn more about how the heart and the blood work with the respiratory system later. The important thing for now

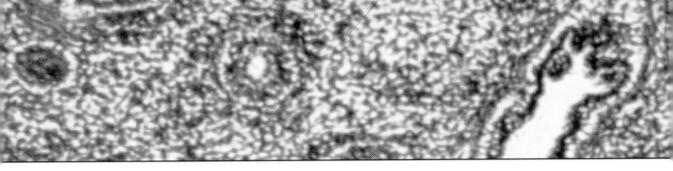

is to understand that your lungs and respiratory system are just one part of a much larger system: your body.

Other Functions of the Respiratory System

Up to this point, we have discussed the way your body manages to keep breathing in and out. When we think of breathing, we primarily think of receiving oxygen, but our respiratory system also allows us to talk. Every time you speak, you use air, and every time you use air, you depend on your respiratory system.

Your vocal cords are located in your larynx—a tube that air passes through on its way to and from your lungs. When we speak, we use air that is pushed out of the body during exhalation. Sound is produced when air makes noise as it passes over our vocal cords and out of our bodies. That noise is formed into words with the mouth and tongue. Singing, screaming, and whispering all depend on this movement of air over the vocal cords. This is why the respiratory system is important to your ability to speak. If your lungs don't work, you can't speak. It's as simple as that.

Laughter is also produced by your respiratory system. When you laugh, your ribs and diaphragm push short, frequent blasts of air up from your lungs, over your vocal cords, and out of your mouth. Try holding your hand over your chest or your stomach as you laugh,

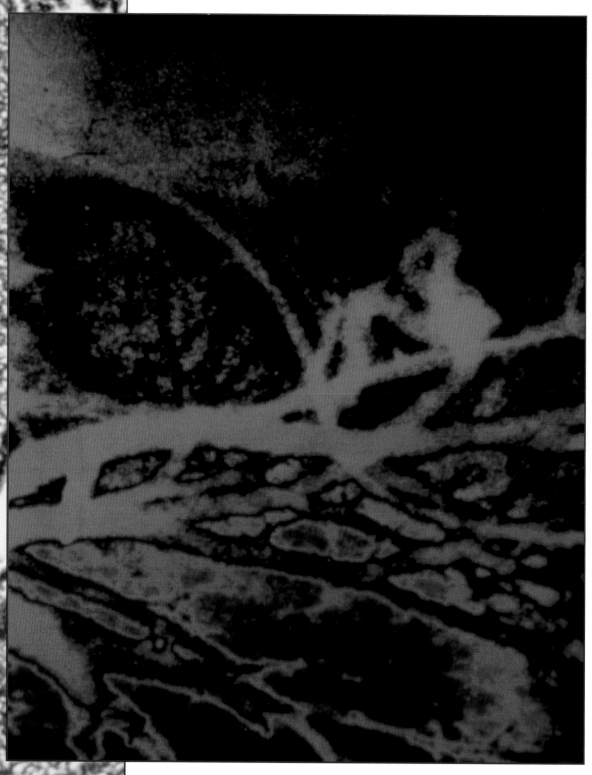

This angiogram shows an abnormality in the pulmonary region.

and you can feel the rhythm of your lungs as they quickly inflate and deflate. Crying works the same way, but you may not want to force yourself to test that.

Two other very important functions of your respiratory system are sneezing and coughing. These two actions are meant to clear germs, mucus, or liquid from the body. When you sneeze, your body is reacting to a stimulus that is coming from your nose. The nerves in your nose tell your brain that there is something that shouldn't be there, whether it be pepper or pollen. The brain sends a message to the respiratory system and that causes you to sneeze. A sneeze is a quick blast of air that travels up and out of the respiratory system. This blast of air is supposed to get rid of any foreign objects. When you sneeze, you blow air out of your nose at more than 100 mph. That is almost twice the legal speed limit on most highways! Coughing works on the same principle, except that it is a response to an irritant in your throat. Smoke can make you cough. So can water, if you swallow it incorrectly.

How the Respiratory System Works

We are all swimming in air. Air covers our entire planet in a thick blanket. The basic problem is that the oxygen that your body needs inside is outside, and the waste that your body needs outside is inside. So how does your body get these things where they need to be? By now you know the answer: Your respiratory system moves them.

Air

Air doesn't just magically show up in your lungs. Your lungs remove oxygen from the air, but before they can do so the air has to travel to the lungs. When the action of your diaphragm and the muscles surrounding your ribs forces your lungs to inflate, a vacuum is created inside the lungs and air rushes in from the outside world to fill that vacuum. Then, when your diaphragm and ribs contract and squeeze your lungs, the same air is pushed back out of you into the world. This process of inhalation and exhalation is how your body makes air come and go.

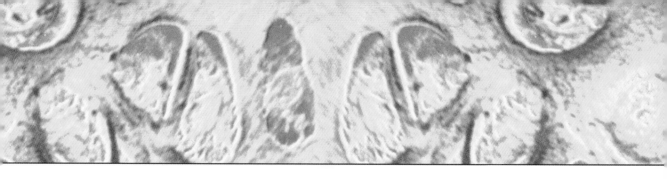

Air travels through the different pipes and tubes in your nose, throat, and chest to reach your lungs. On the way, air is warmed, cleaned, and moistened so that it doesn't hurt the sensitive tissues of the lungs. To understand how air gets to your lungs, it may help to visualize how you get to a friend's house. You take certain roads, and sometimes there is more than one way to get to where you are going. However, you probably have a favorite route—a route that you know and are familiar with. In the same way, the air going to your lungs can go through your mouth or your nose. There is nothing wrong with the mouth route, but the nose route is better. Imagine that when you go to your friend's house there is a safe route with police officers, speed limits, and smooth pavement. There is also a dangerous route with potholes, no speed limits, and no police to keep it safe. The nose is the safe road, with special ways of protecting you and killing germs before they can enter the body. The mouth is the dangerous route because it doesn't have any way to filter the air and keep you safe.

Air travels through your nose, throat, and chest on its way to your lungs. On the way, the air is warmed, cleaned, and moistened so that it doesn't hurt the sensitive tissues of the lungs.

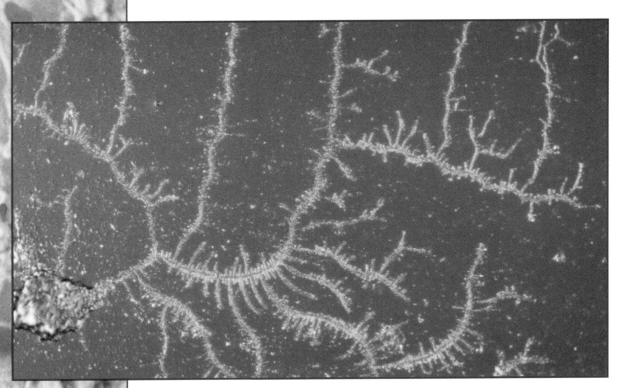

Human mucus "feathers" when a person is sick and has a runny nose.

Your Nose

Air usually enters the body through the nose. Your nose is made of bone and cartilage, and one of its functions is to prepare air for your lungs. The air rushes into your body through your nostrils—the two openings in your nose. Think of your nostrils as the opening of a pipe; then imagine a grate over the pipe that keeps out dead leaves and other kinds of things that might cause clogging. In your body, this grate is actually made up of rough pieces of hair. The hair in your nose stops small pieces of dust and dirt from going into your lungs. The dirt gets caught on these hairs the same way that leaves get stuck on a grate. From there, the dirt is pushed out of your nose when you sneeze or blow your nose.

Cilia

The hair in your nose does a great job of filtering out bits of dirt and dust from the air you breathe in. But some things are too small for the hair to catch, like viruses and bacteria, which can hurt your lungs and body. They have to be taken out of the air as well. To do this, the skin on and in your nose has millions of tiny epithelial cells. Each tiny cell has thousands of microscopic "fingers." These "fingers" are called cilia. The cilia—which through a microscope look like giant beds of seaweed—wave constantly. They are covered in a thick, moist fluid called mucus. In between the tiny cells that are covered with cilia are small goblet cells that produce mucus. Mucus carries away all the dirt, grime, viruses, and bacteria that get caught in your cilia. Instead of going into your lungs, the mucus flows down your throat and into your stomach. There are strong digestive acids in your stomach that break down food. These acids also kill anything that your mucus has in it.

Sometimes there is too much mucus for your stomach to handle. When you get sick your body makes extra mucus. This extra mucus can't all go down into your stomach so some of it runs out of your nostrils. That is why you often have a runny nose when you are sick. The cells that produce mucus also release water vapor. This is important because the air that enters your lungs should have a little water in it so it doesn't dry out your lungs.

Under all of the tiny skin cells that line your nose are thousands and thousands of tiny blood vessels. These blood vessels carry warm blood very close to the skin of your nose. This warmth comes through your skin and makes the air that you

breathe warm, too, so it won't hurt your lungs. When it is cold out, it is harder to warm up the air. Your body has to pump more blood through the blood vessels in your nose. That is why your nose gets red in the cold winter air.

Your nose is the best way for air to get into your body because it does so many things to make the air safe and clean. However, sometimes even the best roads can be blocked. When you get sick your nose can swell shut. Some people have allergies that can block their noses during certain times of the year. Other times, when you are running or exercising very hard, your nose isn't big enough to carry all the air that you need. When these things happen, the air has to take another road. This other road is your mouth.

Your Mouth

Your mouth is like a super highway with no speed limits or safety rules. The air rushes into your mouth and quickly to your lungs. Your mouth does very little to warm, moisten, or clean the air. If you run when it is cold outside, sometimes you have to breathe through your mouth. When this happens, you can actually feel the cold air in your lungs. If it is too cold, you can seriously hurt your lungs by freezing the moisture that is in them. Frozen water, or ice crystals, are very hard. They can tear the soft tissue of your lungs. So the mouth is an alternative route, but the best road for air to take is through your nose.

The human trachea is lined with cilia and goblet cells, shown in blue.
Goblet cells release mucus that traps foreign particles; the cilia propels
the particles to the mouth and nose, where they are expelled.

Similar to the trachea, the internal lining, or epithelium, of the bronchial passages in the human lung is covered with cilia and goblet cells (shown in yellow).

The Pharynx

Once the air is inhaled through your nose, it continues to travel and passes through a tubelike space in your mouth and upper throat called the pharynx. The pharynx is about five inches (thirteen centimeters) long. It is wider at the top than it is at the bottom. Like the nose, it is lined with mucus and cilia. Anything that didn't get caught in the nose can still be filtered out here. The pharynx—where your tonsils are located—has another special feature that helps clean the air. Your tonsils are tissues that hold white blood cells. White blood cells attack viruses, bacteria, and germs. When the air passes over your tonsils, the white blood cells try to kill anything bad that may still be floating around. Sometimes the tonsils lose the battle they are fighting. When this happens, they get swollen and can block your airway.

The Larynx

After passing through the pharynx, air moves into the larynx. The larynx is a tube in the middle of your neck. It is made mostly of cartilage, the same stuff your nose is made of. The larynx is about two inches (five centimeters) long and is tough and flexible. It also has cilia that wave upward and create a small wind that tries to blow any germs out of your body. Your larynx is also important because it is where the vocal cords are located. Your vocal cords allow you to use the air coming out of your lungs to speak, sing, and scream.

Your larynx houses another very important piece of machinery—the epiglottis. The epiglottis looks sort of like a small leaf on the end of a long stem. The epiglottis acts like a door. When you are breathing or speaking, the epiglottis opens and allows air to pass through your larynx. When you swallow food or

water, the epiglottis closes, forcing food and fluids to go down into your stomach through a different tube. When you breathe in, the epiglottis automatically opens, opening the road to the lungs. Your epiglottis works without your even thinking about it. Sometimes, however, it doesn't work the right way. If you laugh while you are swallowing food or water, the epiglottis may not work. When this happens, you can start to choke. Then your lungs respond to your choking and you start to cough—this is what your body does to try to blow the food or water out of your lungs.

The Trachea and Bronchi

Once the air is past the larynx, it is just about clean and ready for your lungs, but it still has to get there. By now it is in your trachea. Your trachea is a wide pipe that is held open by C-shaped rings of cartilage. Your trachea is just below your larynx. It is five to six inches (twelve to fifteen centimeters) long. It is basically a pipe that air travels through. Just below the base of your neck, the trachea splits into two tubes. These tubes are called the bronchi. Each tube takes half of the air. The right bronchus goes to the right lung, while the left bronchus goes to the left lung.

It is important to understand how connected your respiratory system is to the rest of your body. This is especially obvious when you look at the lungs. The right lung is larger than the left lung. The right lung has three lobes, or sections, while the left lung has only two. This is because the left lung has to make room for your heart.

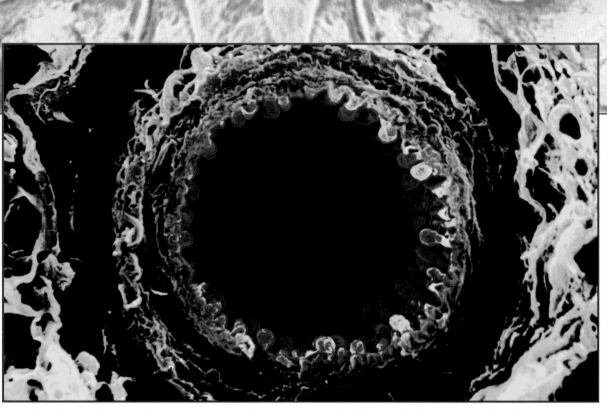

The bronchi are the passages where air travels from the larynx to the lungs.

The Whole Road

Now you know how your body gets air to your lungs. Usually air goes through the nose, but sometimes it has to go through the mouth. Whichever path the air takes, it eventually travels to the lungs via the throat. Occasionally a person will get something stuck in his or her throat that can't be removed. In such an emergency, a doctor will perform an operation called a tracheotomy. During a tracheotomy, a hole is made in the person's throat so that the air can enter the trachea directly. This operation is used only as a last resort to prevent people from choking to death.

Remember, the road the air took to get to the lungs is the same road that it will take when it leaves. It is on the way out that we use the air for speech. If this seems weird, try talking while you are breathing in. It is harder and doesn't sound as good as when you speak with outflowing air.

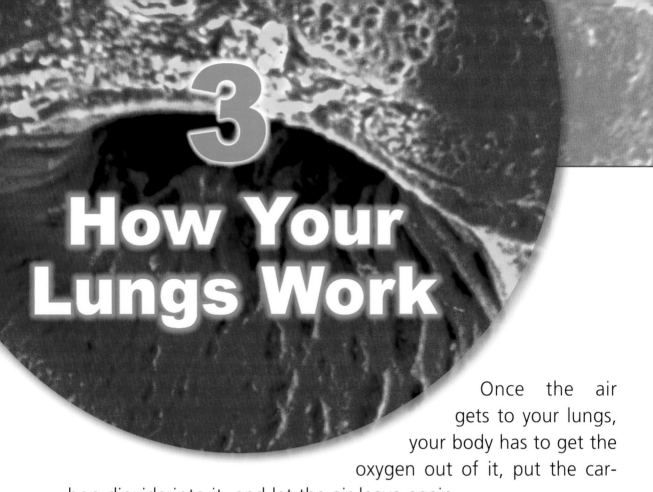

3

How Your Lungs Work

Once the air gets to your lungs, your body has to get the oxygen out of it, put the carbon dioxide into it, and let the air leave again.

The Bronchioles and Alveoli

The right and left bronchi carry the air to the lungs, which are made up of smaller and smaller tubes called bronchioles. The bronchioles are the first part of the lungs that air has contact with. Eventually, the tubes become so small that they are only 0.02 inches (0.5 millimeters) wide. They branch off so many times that they look like the branches of two giant oak trees. The air gets pushed into these tiny tubes and then into the alveoli, which are little sacs located at the ends of the tubes. Once the air reaches the alveoli, its journey into the body is complete. The alveoli are arranged like clumps of grapes. Several of these air sacs group together at the end of each bronchiole. The air fills up these sacs when we breathe in. To give you an idea of how small the alveoli are, try to visualize this: Each lung has about 300 million of them.

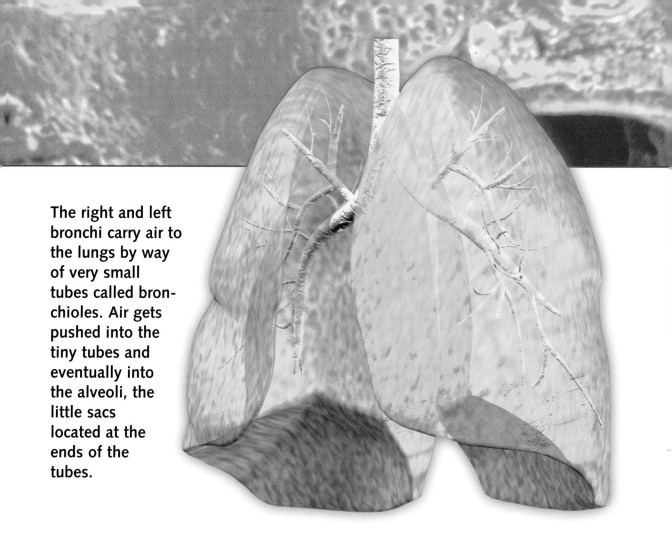

The right and left bronchi carry air to the lungs by way of very small tubes called bronchioles. Air gets pushed into the tiny tubes and eventually into the alveoli, the little sacs located at the ends of the tubes.

Once inside the alveoli, the oxygen leaves the air and enters the blood so it can be carried to all parts of your body. At the same time, the carbon dioxide leaves the blood and enters the air in the alveoli. Then you exhale and the air, now heavy with carbon dioxide, is pushed out of your lungs and starts its return to the outside world.

An Experiment

If you are wondering how much air your lungs can hold, try this experiment. All you need is a balloon. Breathe in deeply. Now hold the balloon to your mouth and exhale a deep breath into it. When you are done exhaling, close off the balloon. That is how much air your lungs hold. Actually, it is a little less than they hold because

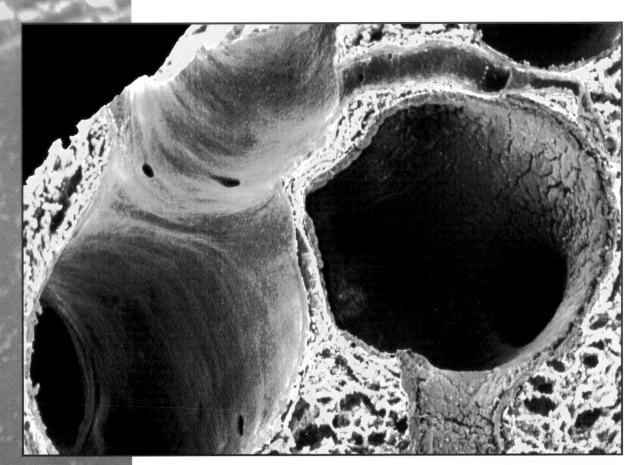

Lung tissue, shown in yellow, is made up of alveoli. Air passes from the bronchi to the alveoli. At right is a bronchus; at left is a blood vessel, through which blood passes.

you can never completely empty your lungs. There is always a little air that doesn't come out.

The Blood

As we have seen, the respiratory system gets air into the lungs and, specifically, into the tiny alveoli. What's the next step? When most people think of lungs they think of air, but the truth is that your lungs are filled with blood as well. The blood comes to your lungs from your heart, which is basically a big pump. This blood is deoxygenated, which means that it doesn't have much oxygen in it and is carrying carbon dioxide. The air that is sitting in your alveoli has very little carbon dioxide and a lot of oxygen. You can already guess the trade that is going to happen.

Basically, the blood system is very much like the bronchioles. The veins that come from your heart start out big and break into smaller and smaller tubes. These tiny tubes that carry deoxygenated blood are called venules. When they get tiny enough they form a net around each bunch of alveoli. At this point they are called capillaries. It is in these capillaries that the blood gets rid of its carbon dioxide and picks up the oxygen. On the way back to the heart, the tubes that carry the newly oxygenated blood are called arterioles.

Gas Exchange

You may be wondering how this gas exchange actually happens. Well, what goes on in the capillaries is that oxygen and carbon dioxide switch places. Let's recap. The air comes in through your nose or mouth. Then it passes through the pharynx, larynx, trachea, bronchi, and bronchioles. Finally it ends up in your lungs in little sacs called alveoli. Meanwhile, the blood has travelled through your body delivering oxygen and picking up the poisonous carbon dioxide gas that your body must get rid of. Then the blood goes all the way to your lungs where it waits patiently inside little tubes called capillaries. These capillaries are spread like tiny nets over bunches of alveoli. At this point, your blood and the air are face to face with each other.

This is where basic physics comes in. All things tend to move from areas of high pressure to areas of low pressure. This sounds complicated but it really isn't. Think about a balloon. As you blow up the balloon, the air inside the balloon is pressurized. When something is pressurized, there is a lot of it in a small, tight area. A balloon gets big because the pressurized air is trying to expand and that makes the balloon bigger. The molecules of air are tightly packed compared to the air outside. Balloons that you blow up fall to the ground because the air inside is heavier and more pressurized. Hence, the air inside the balloon is the high pressure and the regular air outside is low pressure. When you pop the balloon, the air inside immediately spreads out into the regular air instead of remaining as a clump of pressurized air.

This is basic physics. It is like having sixty people in one room and nobody in another room. Because people don't like to be packed together too tightly, some of the people in the room with sixty people will leave and go to the empty room. They go from a place of high pressure to a place of low pressure. When there are thirty people in each room, the pressure will be equal and people will stop moving from room to room. Carbon dioxide and oxygen are the same way. They want to go from high-pressure areas to low-pressure areas.

The gasses inside your alveoli and capillaries function in a similar fashion. In your lungs, blood and air are very close together. The oxygen from the air wants to get into your blood because there isn't a lot of oxygen there; it wants to go to the low-pressure area. The carbon dioxide in your blood is the same way. It realizes that there isn't a lot of carbon dioxide present in the air in your lungs. The carbon dioxide wants to get into the air inside your lungs because it is a low-pressure area. The amazing part is that the walls in between the blood and the air are so thin that they let the gasses pass through them without letting the blood and other air pass through.

Now the blood has its oxygen and the air has its carbon dioxide. The blood goes out of the lungs, back to the heart, and then to the rest of the body to deliver the oxygen that it got in the lungs. Meanwhile, the big muscles of the diaphragm push up and the ribs close tightly around the chest cavity, squeezing the lungs.

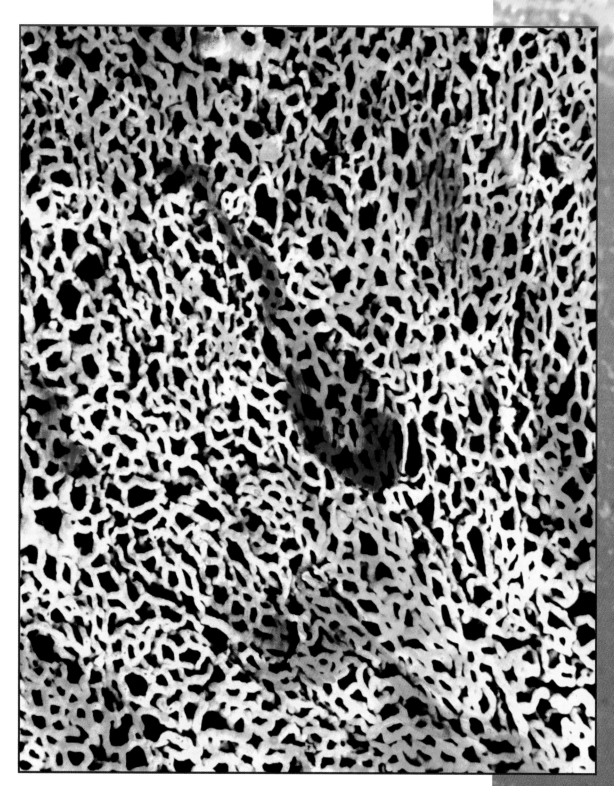

There is a uniform network of capillaries that surround the alveoli, or air sacs of the lungs, responsible for the processing of carbon dioxide and oxygen in the lungs and bloodstream.

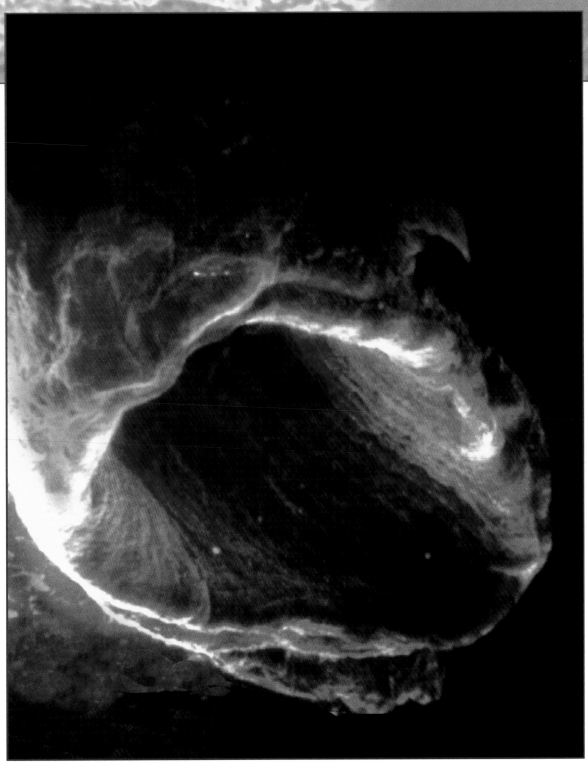

This is a cross section of a vein. Veins are the vessels that carry blood from the capillaries to the heart.

The alveoli inside the lungs are compressed, air is pushed out of the lungs, and the air makes its way out your nose or mouth. The carbon dioxide that the air is carrying is released into air outside the body. This is extremely important, since plants and trees need carbon dioxide to live. In fact, they use the carbon dioxide and push oxygen back into the air—just the reverse of our human process of breathing. You may have noticed that it is easier to breathe in the country than the city. This is because in the country, there are more trees, and more trees means less carbon dioxide and more oxygen.

4
What Can Go Wrong: Respiratory Diseases

To keep you alive, your respiratory system works night and day without a break. Although the respiratory system is amazing, it isn't perfect. Many things can go wrong. Coughing, choking, and sneezing are very normal, and usually the respiratory system fixes small problems like these. Hiccups are a small problem that your respiratory system has to deal with. Hiccups occur when your diaphragm suddenly flattens out causing your chest cavity to expand. This makes you inhale quickly and sharply. The sound a hiccup makes comes from your vocal cords being shut. To stop hiccups, many people suggest things like drinking water from the wrong side of a cup. These remedies are usually more fun to watch than to do!

Getting Sick

Every now and then the mucus, tonsils, and other safety devices in your respiratory system don't catch all the germs that come into your body. When this happens, you can get sick. Bronchitis is a

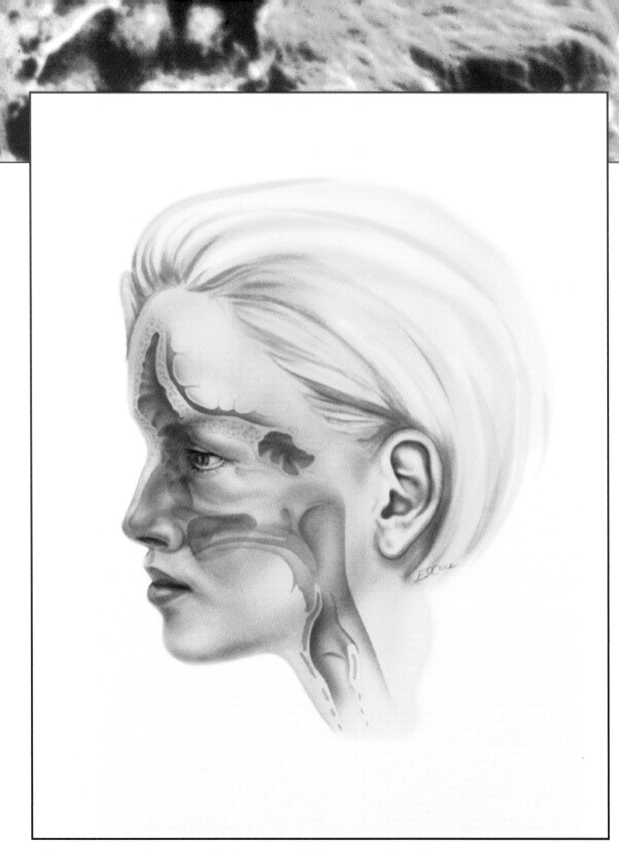

The sinuses are between the larynx and pharynx. When bacteria is
not filtered out of the sinuses, infection can result.

sickness that can affect your respiratory system. As the name suggests, bronchitis occurs when your bronchial tubes get swollen, and the mucus that usually moves freely gets stuck. To get it out of your lungs, your body starts coughing.

Another common disease is influenza, which is caused by a virus. This disease can kill a person if it isn't taken care of. Influenza, or the flu, usually happens during the cold season. There are vaccines for it, but because the virus is able to mutate, or change its form, so quickly, the vaccines can become outdated and ineffective. Pneumonia is another disease that many people get. This sickness is often caused by bacteria that get into the lungs. These bacteria are not that bad by themselves, but when your body gets worn down by being too tired, or because you are sick with some other disease, these bacteria attack. They can cause a lot of irritation in your chest. You can get a sore throat from coughing too much. Pneumonia can even kill you, but in countries where good medical care is available, death from pneumonia is rare among otherwise healthy people.

Disease

There are some respiratory diseases that cannot be cured. These problems don't go away and the people who have them have to learn to live with them.

Asthma

Many people suffer from asthma, a disease that causes the bronchial tubes to constrict and get narrow. It also causes the body to make extra mucus. Together, these two problems can make it very hard for air to get in and out of the lungs. Usually an asthma attack is caused by an allergic reaction to something. When these attacks occur, people who suffer from asthma can use an inhaler to make the tubes in their chests widen out again. Asthma can be scary, but once people know how to deal with it, they can live normal lives.

Cystic Fibrosis

Cystic fibrosis is a disease that isn't curable. You can't catch it. People who have it were born with it. It is horrible because it eventually leads to death. People with this disease make mucus that is very sticky. It gets clogged in their lungs and causes scarring. People with this disease have to take extra care of their lungs.

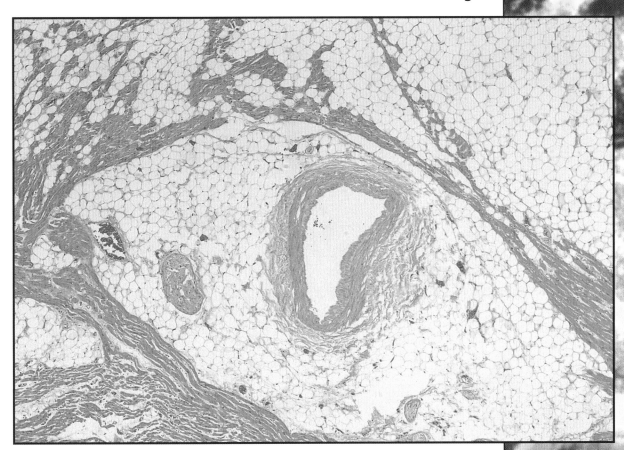

The bronchial tubes of asthma sufferers constrict, meaning that it becomes more difficult to breathe. This is what a constricting bronchial tube looks like.

Cystic fibrosis causes overproduction of mucus in the lungs, which can lead to chronic infections and a reduced lifespan.

Scientists are working hard to figure out a way to cure cystic fibrosis. Even though no cure has been found, doctors and scientists have made many advances in research. Because of this, many people with cystic fibrosis are able to live longer and healthier lives.

Emphysema

Emphysema is a disease that isn't caught or inherited. It is something that we get from the world around us, by breathing poisonous or dirty air or smoking cigarettes. People get emphysema in a number of ways. You can get it from breathing too much smog, or an

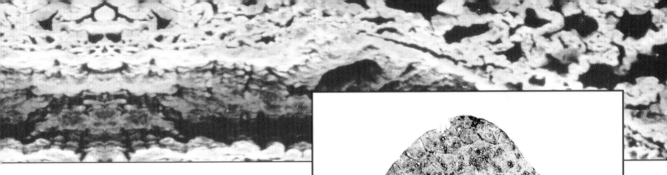

There are other toxins to look out for. If you are around strong fumes or chemicals, wear a face mask. You can buy disposable face masks at most hardware stores. In really hazardous environments, you may want to use a respirator, which is a device that filters air for you. People who work in mines, mills, and factories frequently have a lot of problems with dust in their lungs.

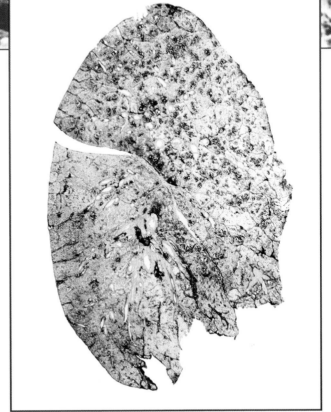

This is a smoker's lung. It is permeated with deposits of tar.

General Care

If you keep your lungs clean and exercise regularly, your respiratory system will stay in good shape. But even the best respiratory systems still get sick. One of the best ways to keep from getting sick is to stay warm in cold weather. If you are going outside, cover your mouth and nose with a scarf, or at least make sure you have warm clothes on. It may not seem like dressing warmly has a lot to do with your respiratory system, but if your body is warm, it is better able to warm the air that comes into it before that air reaches your lungs.

Glossary

alveoli   Little sacs that hold air in the lungs.

arterioles   Small blood vessels that carry blood away from the heart.

bronchi   The divisions of the trachea that carry air to and from the lungs during inhalation and exhalation.

bronchioles   Tiny tubes that are branches of the bronchi.

capillaries   Smallest blood vessels of the body.

cartilage   Body tissue that is strong and somewhat elastic. It is found in the human nose, ears, back, and other areas.

cilia   Tiny, hairlike projections that line the nose.

epiglottis   Thin plate of flexible cartilage that folds over and covers the trachea during swallowing.

epithelial cells   Small cells that line parts of the body.

influenza Highly contagious virus that causes fever, severe aches and pains, and progressive inflammation of the respiratory mucous membranes.

larynx Tube that carries air to the lungs and also houses the vocal cords.

lungs Two spongy, saclike organs in the body that hold air while oxygen and carbon dioxide are exchanged.

mucus Slippery secretion of the body that helps to moisten and protect certain body parts.

pharynx Part of the airway between the nose and the larynx.

respirator Device worn over the mouth or nose to protect the respiratory system.

tonsils Pieces of tissue in the back of the throat that fight infection by catching and killing germs.

trachea Main system of tubes that pass air into the lungs.

tracheotomy Surgical process of cutting into the trachea through the skin so that a person can breathe.

venules Tiny veins that connect capillaries with the larger system of veins.

For More Information

In the United States

American Lung Association
1740 Broadway
New York, NY 10019
(212) 315-8700
Web site: http://lungusa.org

Cystic Fibrosis Foundation
6931 Arlington Road
Bethesda, MD 20814
(800) FIGHT CF (344-4823)
Web site: http://www.cff.org

In Canada

Canadian Cystic Fibrosis Foundation
2221 Yonge Street, Suite 601

Toronto, ON M4S 2B4
(800) 378-CCFF (2233)
Web site: http://www.ccff.ca

Canadian Lung Association
3 Raymond Street, Suite 300
Ottawa, ON K1R 1A3
Web site: http://www.lung.ca

Web Sites

Healthwell
http://www.healthwell.com

How Stuff Works
http://www.howstuffworks.com

KidsHealth
http://www.kidshealth.org

National Institutes of Health (NIH)
http://www.nih.gov

No Tobacco
http://www.notobacco.org

For Further Reading

Bryan, Jenny. *Breathing: The Respiratory System.* New York: Dillon Press, 1993.

Cook, Allen R., and Peter D. Dresser (eds.). *Respiratory Diseases and Disorders Sourcebook.* Detroit, MI: Omnigraphics, 1995.

Hyde, Margaret O. *Know About Smoking.* New York: Walker & Co., 1995.

Parker, Steve. *The Lungs and Respiratory System.* Chatham, NJ: Raintree Steck-Vaughn, 1997.

Sandeman, Anna. *The Children's Book of the Body.* Brookfield, CT: Copper Beech Books, 1996.

Weiss, Jonathan H. *Breathe Easy: Young People's Guide to Asthma.* New York: Magination Press, 1994.

Index

About the Author

Justin Lee lives in New York City. He has a wonderful family and great friends who make sure he keeps breathing in and out.

Photo Credits

Design and Layout